PHRASE BOOK

D0525281

By the same author

Electroplating the Baby (Bloodaxe Books, 1988)

PHRASE BOOK

Jo Shapcott

Oxford   New York

OXFORD UNIVERSITY PRESS

1992

Oxford University Press, Walton Street, Oxford OX2 6DP

Oxford New York Toronto
Delhi Bombay Calcutta Madras Karachi
Petaling Jaya Singapore Hong Kong Tokyo
Nairobi Dar es Salaam Cape Town
Melbourne Auckland

and associated companies in
Berlin Ibadan

Oxford is a trade mark of Oxford University Press

First published in Oxford Poets
as an Oxford University Press paperback 1992

British Library Cataloguing in Publication Data
Data available

Library of Congress Cataloging in Publication Data
Shapcott, Jo, 1953–
Phrase Book / Jo Shapcott.
p. cm.
I. Title
PR6069.H288S6 1992 821'.914—dc20 91–45434
ISBN 0–19–282951–3

Typeset by Rowland Phototypesetting Limited
Printed in Hong Kong

Acknowledgements

Acknowledgements are due to the editors of the following magazines in which some of these poems first appeared: *The Jacaranda Review, Options, Poetry Review, The New Statesman, The Southern Review, The Times Literary Supplement, Verse.* 'Love Song with a Flock of Sheep' won the Prudence Farmer Award for the best poem in *The New Statesman* of 1989. The title poem, 'Phrase Book' was joint winner of the 1991 National Poetry Competition.

In 'A Walk in the Snow' I am indebted to *Ava: My Story by Ava Gardener* (Bantam, 1990).

'The Windows' sequence comes from Rilke's group of fifteen poems in French, *Les Fenêtres* (1927). I wrote three experimental versions, the third of which is published here, and is in what is intended to be a completely new idiom: *after* Rilke.

Some of the poems in this collection are dedicated to friends: 'Love Song with a Flock of Sheep' is for Neil Astley, 'A Walk in the Snow' for Maura Dooley, 'Goat' for Matthew Sweeney, 'Pavlova's Physics' for Sue MacLennan, and 'I'm Contemplated by a Portrait of a Divine' for my students in Cambridge.

Thanks are due to the South Bank Centre, to the Judith E. Wilson Fund of the Faculty of English, University of Cambridge, and to Pembroke College, Cambridge, for generously giving me space and time to finish this book. Special thanks also to the Slovene Writers' Union and the Slovene PEN Centre for offering me hospitality, and to the British Council for supporting my visits to Slovenia.

Contents

I

Tom and Jerry Visit England   3
Pavlova's Physics   5
Brando on Commuting   7
Superman Sounds Depressed   9
Goat   11
Love Song with a Flock of Sheep   12
Vegetable Love   14
I'm Contemplated by a Portrait of a Divine   16
Leonardo and the Vortex   17
Her Lover's Ear   18
Matter   19
Muse   20
The Room   21
On Tour: The Alps   22
Phrase Book   26
In the Bath   28

II

The Windows   31

III

The Mad Cow Talks Back   41
Shopping   42
The Mad Cow in Love   43
Mad Cow Dance   44
Volumes   46
The Mad Cow Tries to Write the Good Poem   47
A Walk in the Snow   48
The Mad Cow Believes She is the Spirit of the Weather   50
Work in the City   51

I

Only the poor cells cannot comment.

> Miroslav Holub, *The Dimension of the Present Moment and Other Essays*

Tom and Jerry Visit England

O boy, I thought. A chance
to visit England and O boy here, out
of nowhere, a voice to describe it. Reader,
I dreamt of coming back to tell you how I marched
round the Tower of London, in a beefeater suit,
swished my axe at Jerry, belted after him
into the Bloody Tower, my back legs
circling like windmills in a gale
while ravens flapped around our heads.
You would hear it all: tea with the Queen
at Buckingham Palace and me scattering
the cucumber sandwiches at the sight
of Jerry by the silver salver. I couldn't wait
for the gorgeous tableau: Queenie with her mouth
in a little shocked screaming shape, her crown
gone crooked as she stood cringing on the throne
with her skirts up round her knees, and Jerry
down there laughing by the footstool.
I would be a concertina zig-zag by that time
with a bone china cup stuffed in my face
.and a floral tea pot shoved on my head so hard
my brains would form a spout and a handle
when it cracked and dropped off.

I can't get this new voice to explain to you
the ecstasy in the body when you fling
yourself into such mayhem, open yourself
to any shape at all and able to throw out
stars of pain for everyone to see.

But reader, the visit wasn't like that.
I ended up in a poem and it made me uneasy.
Cats prefer to skulk and sulk
in the dark, we prefer mystery
and slinking. This is even true of me
with my stupid human face opening
into only two or three stupid expressions:
cunning, surprise and maybe rage.
And I couldn't find Jerry.

'Where's the mouse?' I tripped
over commas and colons hard like diamonds, looking
for him. 'Where's the mouse?' I kept asking,
'Where's the mouse?' I banged full face into a query—
and ended up with my front shaped
like a question mark for hours. That was scary:
I usually pop right back into myself in seconds.
So I hesitated for once before flinging myself
down the bumpy staircase where all the lines ended.
I went on my rear and at the bottom you would have seen me,
end up, bristling with splinters, and nose down
snuffling for any trace of mouse smell.
Reader, it was my first tragic movie:
I couldn't find the mouse.

Pavlova's Physics

Everything in my body
has been processed
through at least one star
(except for the hydrogen).

I want to speak to you about it;
I want you to know how much
I understand—and more and more
reveals itself in waves.

I'm really a wise kid,
the kind that gets on and doesn't
need to go to college to do it,
secretly learning to peel back

the potent leaves of mathematics
while boning up on Greek at night.
For all that, the consciousness
is an outdated barn of a thing,

a slow phenomenon compared
to the speed of the senses.
Today even I'm entranced
by the marine symmetry of my body

but, believe me, this world
is a place of bizarre consequences
where matter can appear
out of nothing and where

the light of stars is ancient
history when it gets here:
we can never understand
what we're living through at the time.

You can show me your piece of warm
thigh the length of Florida
and I'm telling you, I'm affected
by the way you look at me but I need

more dimensions than geography allows.
I'm falling forward, tumbling
into increasing disorder; yes, disorder
is increasing in the universe

and will keep increasing until
the whole shebang becomes a place
where it is remembered
only the alert rodents swam.

Brando on Commuting

It's the knees you notice
on everyone except yourself, but
when you're sitting down you
can't help staring
at the more personal zones
though people blockade them
with what they can: papers,
briefcases, macs. We approach
the lights of the next platform
as tenderly as the big ship
noses the quay.

You think of sex on the tube,
a lot, and you can see the others
do too: nurse lies on a bed
strewn with important documents
her white uniform bunched
round her waist, the papers
sticky and crinkled underneath.
You can't really see the bodies
in the moonlight. Gauguin

and Ligeti are on in London
say the posters across
the track. I like a woman
who understands Gauguin
and Ligeti and I like her
in silk, a vision
sent to me through the grime.

She will be cool, from
a family with a company
about to fly like pirates
on the stock markets
of the world. We'll swim

naked and touch
underwater for what
seems like a year
until I cut through
her shyness like a crusader.

In the heat of the underground
among the rainbow lines
the trains nuzzle the platforms
like fish. They are deaf
and their lives are quiet
and glorious as they take
up and disgorge the litter
of people all along
the flexible length of their bodies.
They run to the cardinal points

of the system: photography
can't snap them in the tunnels
as they crisscross and interweave,
playing like marine mammals.
I think they do the works
down here, present themselves
in courtship colours, each
segment gleaming like ice.

How exactly one services another,
how the glass walls of their sides
stay intact, how they
are prevented from flying
off with their lovers—
if they are prevented,
we could be going anywhere,
for all I know—you just can't tell.
This thing could have sails, or wings
as it commutes, we commute,
I commute, finally rising
away from the scene
on a moving staircase, rising
and admiring the poster art
as I go.

Superman Sounds Depressed

Nothing could have prepared me for this life
in which it all hinges on me,

where it's only me and my past now left
to reassure the world. The trouble is

they forget me fast and start counting
on krill, or thinking they understand

turbulence: so I have to make regular
appearances on the borders

of disaster, dropping through some backdoor
in space whenever I feel the gravity

of their need. Apples for the teacher
are all I get for it, for holding the railway

train on the high viaduct by a single joint
of my little finger, for blowing hard

at the last moment to keep the water upright
in the shape of the shattered dam, for stopping

a model of the earth based on real chaos from
breaking through. I feel spelled all wrong,

stuck in the east wind
with my face caught in an expression

which would mean world financial crisis
if the president wore it. Give me dinner,

a lovely long dinner in dim light, with someone,
someone who will propose something rude

so it doesn't sound rude—just delicious—
nothing personal, anxious or brutal about it

though it might seem all of those things
to others when it's not night, over their ordinary

sandwiches: wholemeal, mustard
and fragile morsels. My head aches; I want

that woman and enough passion to blast away
any hope of understanding what's happening

to me. And I want us to eat scallops,
and I want to lick the juice from her chin

as though I could save the world that way,
and I won't even ask what passion is for.

Goat

Dusk, deserted road, and suddenly
I was a goat. To be truthful, it took
two minutes, though it seemed sudden,
for the horns to pop out of my skull,
for the spine to revolutionize and go
horizontal, for the fingers to glue
together and for the nails to become
important enough to upgrade to hoof.
The road was not deserted any more, but full
of goats, and I liked that, even though I hate
the rush hour on the tube, the press of bodies.
Now I loved snuffling behind his or her ear,
licking a flank or two, licking and snuffling here,
there, wherever I liked. I lived for the push
of goat muscle and goat bone, the smell of goat fur,
goat breath and goat sex. I ended up on the edge
of the crowd where the road met the high
hedgerow with the scent of earth, a thousand
kinds of grass, leaves and twigs, flower-heads
and the intoxicating tang of the odd ring-pull
or rubber to spice the mixture. I wanted
to eat everything. I could have eaten the world
and closed my eyes to nibble at the high
sweet leaves against the sunset. I tasted
that old sun and the few dark clouds
and some tall buildings far away in the next town.
I think I must have swallowed an office block
because this grinding enormous digestion tells me
it's stuck on an empty corridor which has
at the far end, I know, a tiny human figure.

Love Song with a Flock of Sheep

'Win a flock of sheep' said the advertisement.
'Sheep Dip: an eight year old pure malt whisky.
You will find an entry form on every bottle.'

I will. I will buy the whisky,
I will find the entry form. I will:
I will win the sheep and I'll give them to you.

Keep the flock at home
and let them graze around the house.
Kindly and damp, they'll eat the carpet
and will start on the wallpaper too,
your interior decorations will be masticated away.
The flock is softer than soft furnishings
but when they've eaten all that they'll start
on the hard stuff. They'll munch their way
through the mantelpiece and everything—
your books, your manuscripts—
will fly into their placid mouths.

I know you. You'll like it better without
all that ruminated stuff. You want
the woolly life, carding and spinning,
with only sheep for furniture and bedclothes.
The flock will find you out eventually
and start their blowing in your ears
and their nuzzling across your hair.
It will begin in the kitchen with a fleecy
brush along the backs of your knees.
They'll surround you on the sofa
and drink out of your bath. Your clothes
will go into the three stomachs and in the dark
you'll feel sheep nibble between your toes
and suck your toenails. They will graze
your legs, removing every hair with teeth
so precise and shy you'll feel only
a mist of breath and lips. They'll move
in a cloud across your chest, your belly,

face and beard—everywhere—cropped
down to a downy stubble, peaceful as pasture.
Soon you will be as shorn as a yearling lamb
and twice as happy, blissoming with the flock.

When I arrive, dressed as Bo-Peep,
I won't get a look in. But by hook or by crook
you shall have them anyway: sheep fleecy, sheep shorn
and me lovelorn.

Vegetable Love

I'd like to say the fridge
was clean, but look at the rusty
streaks down the back wall
and the dusty brown pools
underneath the salad crisper.

And this is where I've lived
the past two weeks, since I was pulled
from the vegetable garden.
I'm wild for him: I want to stay crunchy
enough to madden his hard palate and his tongue,
every sensitive part inside his mouth.
But almost hour by hour now, it seems,
I can feel my outer leaves losing resistance,
as oxygen leaks in, water leaks out
and the same tendency creeps further
and further towards my heart.

Down here there's not much action,
just me and another, even limper, lettuce
and half an onion. The door opens so many,
so many times a day, but he never opens
the salad drawer where I'm curled in a corner.

There's an awful lot of meat. Strange cuts:
whole limbs with their grubby hair,
wings and thighs of large birds,
claws and beaks. New juice
gathers pungency as it rolls down
through the smelly strata of the refrigerator,
and drips on to our fading heads.

The thermostat is kept as low as it will go,
and when the weather changes
for the worse, what's nearest
to the bottom of the fridge starts to freeze.
Three times we've had cold snaps,
and I've felt the terrifying pain
as ice crystals formed at my fringes.

Insulation isn't everything in here:
you've got to relax into the cold,
let it in at every pore. It's proper
for food preservation. But I heat up
again at the thought of him,
at the thought of mixing into one juice
with his saliva, of passing down his throat
and being ingested with the rest
into his body cells where I'll learn
by osmosis another lovely version
of curl, then shrivel, then open again to desire.

I'm Contemplated by a Portrait of a Divine

I cannot speak to you. My lips are fused
where an archangel kissed them. I have never
made much of myself although I know,
sometimes, that space is touching me
because I have seen the crack in the universe
through which the galaxies stream. O God,
I will always know how to walk, no rest, until
it just ends in blackness when I fall down flat.
I have one arching eyebrow: my whole life
is in that eyebrow where an angel nestles
at the root of every hair, raising it up.
Dear Christ, I can hear vice rushing through
the grass. There is someone here.
If I could lick the glass
clean from this side, I might see her, though
I already know she would look the way
I want my soul to look. This pose
which I strain to keep, in which I lean
on the desk for dear life, is not a pose.
It's so important for keeping the drawer shut
in case my heart should slip out, fly up.

Leonardo and the Vortex

I get like him sometimes:
seeing the same shape in everything
I look at, the same tones
in everything I hear.

But I'll never make a deluge drawing
or be gripped by the science of circular
motion. And I probably won't learn to care how
many complex collisions happen in a pool
when water is trickled from above.
How currents percuss against each other,
and how waves rebound into the air, falling
again to splash up more water in smaller
and smaller versions of the same.
How a storm is different where air and water mix,
bursting again and again through the thin skin
which separates them. How a woman's hair
moves in spouts and spirals just like water
and how the leaves of the star plant
trail on the ground in a loose coil.
And look at your sleeve, folding and swirling
around your arm, and the pattern of fine black hairs
curving from your inner wrist to your outer elbow,
and the underlying muscles relying on that slight
twist around the lower arm for their strength,
and the blood coiling around your body
through the little eddies in the larger veins
and arteries, coiling towards the vortex
in the chambers of your heart where I sit,
where the impetus has pulled me in.

Her Lover's Ear

I woke up as a flying speck in the sunshine
which bothered me for a while, because I missed you,
though whirling in the air was a thrill.
I zoomed along the breeze tracks,
learning to accelerate into gravity,
floating up at the last by hitching
on to a draught from the door crack.
But nobody notices a mote, so, bored,
I moved into calmer air. Even here
there were surges and lulls which
buffeted me around—waves of sound
rocking me towards your ear.

Everywhere on the body, touch makes sound
but the ear is the one place
you can't tell them apart,
where even the noise of a fingertip
rustles and explodes.

I was glad to see you:
I thought I might know in my human life
how to touch you lightly
after this rehearsal as a piece of dust.

I tripped against your lobe
just so you would know I was there,
and felt the fine hairs rise in the notch above.
As the air pushed me round the helix,
I leaned outwards on the bend like a biker
so I could press against the rim
in a long brush as the air flowed past
just gritty enough for you to feel.
Swept into the bowl of the concha
I felt you move as I tickled against
your skin and skidded softly
with the momentum into your skull.

Matter

He touched my skin
all afternoon
as though he could feel
the smallest particles
which make me up.

By tea time he knew each
of the billions of electrons
which fly through my body
every second.

Then I think he was searching
for the particles
not yet discovered
but believed to exist.

Then I didn't know
what time it was any more
and neither of us knew
which was inside or outside
as he reached somewhere
very deep and fingered gold—
charms, stranges, tops and gravitons—
but not the words he wanted
which only come now.

Muse

When I kiss you in all the folding places
of your body, you make that noise like a dog
dreaming, dreaming of the long runs he makes
in answer to some jolt to his hormones,
running across landfills, running, running
by tips and shorelines from the scent of too much,
but still going with head up and snout
in the air because he loves it all
and has to get away. I have to kiss deeper
and more slowly—your neck, your inner arm,
the neat creases under your toes, the shadow
behind your knee, the white angles of your groin—
until you fall quiet because only then
can I get the damned words to come into my mouth.

The Room

She gives a fingernail clipping
to the naked man.
It will fly up
and amaze him
when she's gone.

He balances it
on his belly:
it's light and dry.

The noisy thing.
He is sure
he can hear
it speaking
as he grazes
it softly all over
his skin.

On Tour: The Alps

But today the sun shines as we arrive
at the highest point, and my bloke's grumbling
that a pass is a strange place to stop. No one
else sleeps over he says—other tourists pause

for a beer, a photograph or two and head on,
to Italy the one way, to Switzerland the other.
Only hikers and a smattering of soldiers
have made up reasons to stay. Ah. Breathe.

Ignore him. We're at the very heart of Europe,
a place where everyone's a traveller, moving: last century
Byron passed in his rattling coach, purpose-built
for European tours. I imagine its special

fittings, pure James Bond: the walls
inside are soft, padded velvet, crimson and you
sink into the seats so it's difficult to get up.
They are slightly too narrow and the coach's sway

round Alpine hairpin bends pitches you against
your neighbour's shoulder or if things are really going
his way, into his lap. Does a cabinet of drinks
swing out of the mahogany panel? Do the seats

collapse at the touch of a button to throw you
wriggling on your back? The carriage rollocks
along, mountain scenery passes in a blur
and I'm falling for Byron's smile, his charming

weaknesses, his warm coach, the springs
squeaking and bouncing, horses'
breath steaming away into the mountain night fog.
There's enough madness in me to fall,

enough to spare for a smile as the carriage
slows and I'm flung out at dawn,
dumped on my rear by a roadside
in the Alpine foothills, Italy or Switzerland,

or some other country where no one speaks
a language I know, and the back of the coach lurches
round curves into the distance where
I can hear, I think, the amazing tang of cowbells.

⁓

Could be I'm just remembering it from higher up
where, let's all come back down to earth, I really am.
Breathe in, yes, our party's at the top of the pass,
and listen, amidst the true sound of cowbells,

the tourists, the climbers, the smattering of soldiers.
We're guided here by my lover's bad temper,
and my panic to settle him in an astonishing spot
because there's all Europe to pick on, and we

desperately want to get him peachy again,
to get the mean spider out of his brain where
it's sat all day, spoiling. And I feel
responsible: it's my continent on show.

We climbed here in a Volvo but the mountain museum
tells us Wordsworth walked all the way, proud
to be pedestrian. I could have done that too,
could have matched him step for step

even in the snow. Everywhere a new pathway,
and I'm there with him, to help turn walking
into statement, more than just somewhere to go. We talk
politics as much as topography and I help him

by thinking legs, not imagination
so we can do twenty, sometimes thirty miles
a day, even in this mountain territory.
I watch him stride off-scene towards

imagined terrible peaks, leaving me
a scrap of local colour in the dark, set
against herds you can't see but hear
in soft clangs as they move through the mist.

⁓

The inn's homely, smells of wood and climbers'
leather, canvas; my lover's pleased that beer
and wurst is generous, cheap. Note the tremendous
view across the pass from our room, only

the evening fog's come down with a vengeance
and we're sitting in thick cloud. The walls
are dark pine and the ceiling painted
with animals, ladies, lovely scenes you want to be in,

in a way, but not so tied down. Later, in the bar,
the receptionist stares at my lover while
she whispers to me in German about Goethe,
how he stayed here for his geology

to make a study of the mountain stones.
Sweet Goethe, picking among the minerals—
I could spot them just as smartly, find
something precious for his delectation,

chuckle as he rolls little boulders towards
my feet, piles them between my legs. Look at me
supervising sacks of rocks, naming and weighing
just like him, testing and cataloguing too.

હ

The bed's huge, the way around it tight.
We have to make complicated choices,
who's to get in, out: one of us is always in the way.
High off the ground, too, that bed, a real clamber

and all night a background fear of the drop to the floor.
The room, the bed, the cloud, the view, give my lover
dreams until dawn. For hours he mutters and groans
a stack of nouns—names of stars, of women, of things

in the world outside our wooden box. And the room starts
to lose its charm for me as my mind too drifts
outside towards the dark up there somewhere
above the mountain fog, towards the muffled stars.

Beneath the huge down quilt, a mountain
in itself, I'm wondering, as I reach to comfort him,
about love—how it lets in the whole world,
even the cloud sitting on the mountain top,

the awfulness of the stars we can't see,
the animals, walkers, cars rolling
across the pass, the very dark itself and
I want it to be daytime, I badly want not to listen

to him shouting now in his dreams he's had
enough, calling out names I don't know. I want to jump
into the car and coast him down to the lakes,
where it will be different and in the mornings

I can bring fresh raspberries from the market.
And we do leave, after breakfast, we do,
but even as far as Lucerne I'm listening
for the strange clang that tells you

mountain animals are on the move
only it's hard to tune my ear to it
against so many men's voices shouting
all the names they know, at the dark.

Phrase Book

I'm standing here inside my skin,
which will do for a Human Remains Pouch
for the moment. Look down there (up here).
Quickly. Slowly. This is my own front room

where I'm lost in the action, live from a war,
on screen. I am an Englishwoman, I don't understand you.
What's the matter? You are right. You are wrong.
Things are going well (badly). Am I disturbing you?

TV is showing bliss as taught to pilots:
Blend, Low silhouette, Irregular shape, Small,
Secluded. (Please write it down. Please speak slowly.)
Bliss is how it was in this very room

when I raised my body to his mouth,
when he even balanced me in the air,
or at least I thought so and yes the pilots say
yes they have caught it through the Side-Looking

Airborne Radar, and through the J–Stars.
I am expecting a gentleman (a young gentleman,
two gentlemen, some gentlemen). Please send him
(them) up at once. This is really beautiful.

Yes they have seen us, the pilots, in the Kill Box
on their screens, and played the routine for
getting us Stealthed, that is, Cleansed, to you and me,
Taken Out. They know how to move into a single room

like that, to send in with Pinpoint Accuracy, a hundred Harms.
I have two cases and a cardboard box. There is another
bag there. I cannot open my case—look out,
the lock is broken. Have I done enough?

Bliss, the pilots say, is for evasion
and escape. What's love in all this debris?
Just one person pounding another into dust,
into dust. I do not know the word for it yet.

Where is the British Consulate? Please explain.
What does it mean? What must I do? Where
can I find? What have I done? I have done
nothing. Let me pass please. I am an Englishwoman.

In the Bath

She was interested in prehistory.
It didn't seem so long ago and offered
pleasant notions of a time before civic duty,
when disease was accepted and fought through,
or not. Hers wasn't a museum interest:
it was as tight, neat and uncomplicated
as a reef knot. 'If I came here as a visitor
from Mars, I would be impressed by the water,
the relative health of the inhabitants, the indecent
urge of atoms for complexity—they don't just split
once, think they're clever, and then stop.' She imagined
her body cells spreading like a film to cover the earth,
coating every frond in the tropical rain forest,
every blade of grass on the pampas. Herself
spread thin and making the surface of the world
sparkle. It was a stunning vision of the future.
She lay in the bath with the water touching
her all over, and remembered that not even
the most tender lover could do that. She wondered
if every molecule on the surface of her skin
was wet and what wet meant to such very
tiny matter. To make things worse, or at least
more difficult for the water, she raised her body
slightly, building an island chain of hip bones,
belly, breasts all of which began to dry at once.
She loved the water trails over her body curves,
the classical lines between wet and dry
making graph patterns which she thought might follow
the activity in her brain—all she wanted
was to be a good atlas, a bright school map
to shine up the world for everyone to see.

II

The Windows
after Rilke

Jezt wär es Zeit, das Götter träten aus
bewohnten Dingen . . .

(Now it is time that gods came walking out
of lived-in things . . .)

Rainer Maria Rilke

The Windows

after Rilke

I

It's enough that all the things
around are more real than anything else,
more real than me. The furniture, balcony,
doors, the windows, I spoke to them
and they talked back.

Then a woman, shy, came into the picture
and the windows flattened back into the walls,
the bits of furniture sat down again on the carpet.
Her arms, hair, smell made the dead things
quiet again, but I knew I would lose her too.

II

I won't stop talking to you just because
you're acting strange. You mouthed off
all day yesterday, blinds flapping in the breeze
and now, not a peep out of you, and
the thin curtain only just moving.

I'm waiting, listening, could wait all day;
it doesn't diminish me to look a fool
with my cheek against the glass for hours.
I've got time and time and a triumphant soul
because you'll crack eventually
and let me through or let me in.

III

Talking to you like this
makes everything clear.
The lines that make up the world
show up so I can understand them.

A woman may be beautiful
but I can even tolerate that
when you put yourself
between us, making us look.

No chance that who I am
can get lost in this space,
small, airy, like love
with me in the middle.

IV

It's true, I do talk to you more
when I'm drunk, the chair pulled up close,
my forehead and the glass in my hand
pressed against the pane.

My nose is so
close up I can see
the separate pores
as drops on the surface.

So there's me, my face at least,
but all the time the shadow
of something else, the dirt
on the glass, the big mess outside.

V

I feel as if you've made me up.
Here is time, framed,
wearing a jacket that's too big,
draped like a child.

Once I leaned and stayed so long
I looked different: more of a child
with fewer lines, but it was getting light outside
and the sun drains the detail from the glass.

I think I want you to save me from love
but then it arrives here too
in the wrong mood, beating
against my forehead with wings.

VI

I do want love deep down, somewhere in the back
of my spine.
I watch the window now as if she were a woman
stretching the stars
into dawn, everything a lover must know.
She's mean,
early on, but I like that, it gets me ready
for the sun's explosion
when my eyes don't know what to do
with all that
after the different abandon of the night.

Maybe there's nothing there after all
except the air
but I'm sure the sky must be made of more,
the way the birds
seem to hold on to it, the way they move
their feathers,
the way they measure it, taste it, fuck it
as they fly.

VII

I'm starting to count you now
as though you might hide with the others
around the room if I once
lost track of the numbers.

Did I sit on the sill, or was it
someone I knew, spending hours there,
so it seemed, trying to touch
the one I didn't love with meaning.

I'm drunk again, you know,
so drunk it all gets clearer
for a second, until I see myself, bent
at the waist, falling down blind.

VIII

Is it her dream or mine?
When I invite her home now
she sits near you, leaning.
Forearms, breasts, shoulders.

It's true she's beautiful
and knows how to place
herself just so, especially
her long hands on the glass

and the rest tense as if
she wanted to jump right through.
She's not enough, although
I might think so if she did go.

IX

O boo hoo, O shame.
Window, your skin's wet inside
from my tears and wet
outside with rain.

We've got this close
too late, too soon;
now I'm dressed up in curtains,
voile, organdy, void.

X

Woman, yes, I'm talking
to you now, and I'm watching
you lean out of that window
doing it to make me nervous.

You're a poser;
with your beautiful arms up
and your head turned
you give yourself away.

I don't understand gestures
in the dark, the way you use
the window as a backdrop
and me as the blind audience.

XI

I can't help it, I taste
whatever you have to offer.
You taste of night and day.
You taste of all the weathers.

Maybe that's everything, maybe
nothing, all show for the eyes
keeping me awake in case
I miss something wonderful.

Promises, promises; and all the while
the world shrivels in front of me.
I'm tired and still my eyes gobble roses
rainforests, oceans, satellites, the moon.

XII

I'm in the mood for gardening.
I look carefully for the subtle lichens
spreading tiny hairs on the outside frame
and even on the glass at the edge.

Small insects, aeroplanes brush by our field
of vision, birds do, and clouds. I study
each flight path and trajectory across
the small square, study hard and memorize.

I'm soothed by what's out there, the force
of it. I can watch all day, you know I can,
close as a breath to you but never touching.
Why? In order to see how to get out.

XIII

Now she's looking hard, watching hard.
The microscope stance by the window. It's
embarrassing to see her concentrate this hard
as though it could help her soul meet the world.

I daren't even glance at her now because I think
I would see right through her eyes to the coils
of her brain. A better man might say her look
watered a sweet garden of images, but it's just not true.

You see, her heart, her heart's just not in it—
too busy counting the number of beats spent
and balancing the total against what's left
so we can calculate what her name is when she's gone.

XIV

I'm a sod in the morning, and so are you, sky
up there, all square, mouthing things at me
and licking the room till it's worn out,
till it sticks out its tongue at you, in return:
two great liars wagging their tongues at each other—
then at me. And watch what you say about me,
or I'll beat you up, I'll beat all the bad tongues;
you say it again and again, you keep talking about
the fall, the rug, the dirty drop into bed.

XV

I'm just playing around, window,
fooling my own eyes and you
when I want so much to translate
us both up into the sky.

You've pulled out of me a final form
which comes through you or from you.
There's a crack in the corner
where the putty is loose.

I want to climb and see you
climb too into a new constellation.
You, window, and you, stars, and me,
I want us all to be rhymes.

III

Und in dieser Unwirklichkeit: Tiere: das Wirklichste von allem.

(And in all this unreality: animals—the realest of all.)

Rainer Maria Rilke, letter to Clara Rilke

O dieses ist das Tier, das es nicht giebt.
Sie wußtens nicht und habens jeden Falls
—sein Wandeln, seine Haltung, seinen Hals,
bis in des stillen Blickes Licht—geliebt.

(Oh this is the animal that never was.
They hadn't seen one; but just the same, they loved
its graceful movements, and the way it stood
looking at them calmly, with clear eyes.)

Rainer Maria Rilke, *Sonnets to Orpheus*
tr. Stephen Mitchell

The Mad Cow Talks Back

I'm not mad. It just seems that way
because I stagger and get a bit irritable.
There are wonderful holes in my brain
through which ideas from outside can travel
at top speed and through which voices,
sometimes whole people, speak to me
about the universe. Most brains are too
compressed. You need this spongy
generosity to let the others in.

I love the staggers. Suddenly the surface
of the world is ice and I'm a magnificent
skater turning and spinning across whole hard
Pacifics and Atlantics. It's risky when
you're good, so of course the legs go before,
behind, and to the side of the body from time
to time, and then there's the general embarrassing
collapse, but when that happens it's glorious
because it's always when you're travelling
most furiously in your mind. My brain's like
the hive: constant little murmurs from its cells
saying this is the way, this is the way to go.

Shopping

I approved of it heartily, the multiway underwired bra
from the Pearls Collection in lots of nonstandard sizes.
I took it to try. Next groceries, and maybe a plant or two,
something green and exotic enough to refresh my system,
to help me imagine the place off-shore
where I recently stashed my savings. You could
exchange it too, the multiway bra, if it didn't fit:
a serious life or time consideration. I am mostly
vegetarian and skitter up the supermarket aisles
pursuing my health. What goes in that basket is important.
I like it to be from the country, something that had a green
and happy life once, that knew hope and had a generous
and juicy nature. You can't make deals with your stomach
about the future. I try to avoid this craze and that craze
but if you're going to delay death and stay in your prime
week in week out you have to make the hard choices
of the supermarket. Salivating over the loin chops
in the freezer and still passing by equates with goodness
or at least good sense which is the nearest we can get to it
at this time, halving the odds on immediate decay, keeping
a firm straight back well into middle age, the signal
that you want something badly or want something badly not
to happen, because should it happen you're never ready
these days, days of oils, marks and time.

The Mad Cow in Love

I want to be an angel and really think
I'm getting there with this mind of mine,
shrinking every day towards the cleanness,
the size of a baby animal's brain.
Trouble is, I want you to be an angel too
—and want that more if anything. It's one
of those demands I can't raise just like that,
evenings, when we're reading our different newspapers
you scanning your pages and me mine for an item
to start speech, make mouths smile, knees touch—something
in all that murder and mayhem to launch love.
You tell me you're looking for news of the self.
Do you want to be an angel? I know
the answer already and it's rough medicine.
But think of all the kinds there are, as many
as the different degrees of reaching
for the good. You might get away without
searching for the soul at all in those places,
today at least, you'd rather not get to know.
And angels do a variety of jobs:
the post of perpetual adoration might suit,
or divine messenger but I fancy for you
the government of the stars and all the elements.
I know you well enough to choose, after all this time
as foreign correspondent on the track of who you are,
looking for leads: your last screw, the food
you threw away, your strategic approaches
for living through the next hour. I don't mean it,
though, any of it. I want you earthly,
including all the global terrors and harms
which might come when we fall backwards
into the world of horn and hoof.

Mad Cow Dance

I like to dance. Bang. I love to dance. Push.

It makes me savage and brilliant. Stomp. To
my own rhythm, rhythm. I lead or I don't

have a partner. No market for partners,
just this wide floor for the dance.
I think I was born here. Swoop. I don't care.

Even if I'd been born in the back of a car

the chassis and each blessed spring
would have jumped as I leapt out

of my mum. Up. Down to the ocean, perhaps
the beach? Hah. Stone steps and stone walls,
the pebbled strand, try to stall my special

high-kicks for the sea. But fireflies

know I'm here, raving with light,
they swirl down my spine. Swish. My tail

goes bam, thwack against the backs
of my legs. Pleasure, local pleasure.
Listen, sitting-down reader, I reckon

faces would be red if you knew what

was next. The little fibres
of my muscles give me such a charge.

Bread and butter. Release. Ceasefire
between my legs and my brain. Sweet oil
flows down to my little hooves. I like

to turn and call to my friends in

northern towns: kick out, kick back, fruity,
for a second. We can meet among characters

who don't dance, and hoof it till dawn, gas
on and on even when we're moving the most.
Four legs increase splits into splats,

just watch me

become
pure product, pure

use,
pure perfume,
jasmine and fucked.

Volumes

They put me in a fever. It's not enough
to look. I want to hold them all
and stuff them in the gaps in my head.
I gallop past Health towards Travel
where I break into a muck sweat
as I lift and sniff a book about Verona.
The odour makes me stagger and long
to be a book mite, to live right inside
and gulp holes through the picture maps.
I don't trust myself in Fiction. The thought
of those thousands and thousands of stories—
the crush and babble of other minds—
makes the whites of my eyes show and roll.
Last time I sauntered by those shelves
I slammed into the New Titles display
and crashed right through a pyramid of books
on to my back among the toppled photos
of authors winking at the carry on.
I got a cuppa and a pat on the rump
from the kind saleslady who has the bubble
of book hysteria herself, I'd guess.
If she could, she'd wear print on her skin.
There are words written for everything,
I think, and it's only a matter of time
before I find a new 'How To' book:
how to stand upright, how not to fall
and how not to cry out when you do.

The Mad Cow Tries to Write the Good Poem

The police came once when I was doing my death dance
to the amazing circular music which had entered a gap
near my cortex and acted as powerfully as a screwdriver
on my soul. I wove in and out of the green trees. I used
my hooves as gentle weapons in the air. A bit of newspaper
fame came my way that day, but shit, it was a performance
ephemeral, and certainly not the good poem. Lasting.
How can I last when I live in a shed and even
the postman doesn't know how to find me?
It's dark in here. Light would echo the gaps
in my brain coils and set off a fizzing reaction,
not so much pounding, more an explosion
followed by a flowing moment when the taboo
people arrive. They're dressed in red and
stand formally around my skull as though staged
for an opera. And when they sing—sometimes as many
as seven at once—then, friend, please, the good
poem is sounding all round this hut, my head, the world,
I hear it written in the streaky emulsion on the walls,
in my own messing on the floor, in the nation's smeary dailies,
in lovely people's ears, their breath, your breath:
it's new every time, always wanted and easy to spot
because I know what it looks like with my eyes closed.

A Walk in the Snow

There's something shameless about
snowfall, the way it lies there,
does nothing but changes everything.
So when freak storms hit London

I couldn't resist all that cleanness;
the glitter on the street outside
made me salivate, the dazzle
and glamour on our ordinary road.

I tottered out with Deirdre, sliding—
sliding worst of all where ice
was topped by snow. We hung on
to each other. I don't know who hung

more or hung on longer, while we rocked
with laughter and those sharp movements
the upper body makes to stay upright.
Breathless like that you talk too loudly,

as though the volume's been turned right up.
Everything's too big—the rhythm of your body
too large, too loud in the effort to keep
your torso pointed straight down the pavement,

your legs true to where you want to go.
We were heading for the park, and we made it,
but left ourselves too tired even to think
about the end. The helpless feeling made us laugh

until I fell on my back in the snow,
my breath, the laughter and the cold air
bursting in my chest as I lay there.
Sick, dizzy and squinting in the sunshine

I looked up to see a spread of branches
filled with frost, every twig cluttered
with wings, haloes, stars. Deirdre
plonked herself next to me and of course,

after we'd sat there we couldn't get up.
We had to roll over and over towards
the nearest tree, crawling the last part.
A stupid dog, the small sort, found us

and jumped and snuffled and yapped until I said,
'If the fucker would shut up, everybody
wouldn't see us.' We edged close enough
to the tree for Deirdre to pull herself up,

then she reached out for me. We were laughing
so hard water was running down our legs and I said,
'Deirdre, did you ever think we would come to this?'
And she said, 'No, never, never, never.'

The Mad Cow Believes She is the Spirit of the Weather

People out walking lean into the wind, the rain:
they believe it thwarts the weather to welcome it like that.
I can happily get lost for hours in a swirl of showers
because I was born into weather. They still tell
how my mother pushed me out of her body
on to a rock and I split the stone in two while the rain
washed me and the thunder broke overhead.
I was a junior cloud goddess, with storms following
me, winds and whirlwinds, shots of rain
and a split sky above my head. Always moving,
I kept one jump ahead of getting wet, kicking
back at the clouds with my hind legs
to keep them there. It's harder now, here
in the future: my brain has the characteristics
of a sponge and the rain seeps into the holes.
I think I'm making chaos. My vests
don't keep me warm and when I last sneezed
a volcano in the Pacific threw a sheet of dust
around the world. I'm dangerous to the earth.
I spat and a blanket of algae four miles long
bloomed on the Cornish coast. I rubbed
the sleep from my eyes and a meteor large enough
to make the earth wobble in its orbit
came very close indeed. I have been sad recently
and now the weather has changed for good.

Work in the City

Yes I do hold down a job and I find
the air in my brain helps combat
the stress. Once, carrying
my lunch back to the office, the tea
steaming in a polystyrene cup, the roll crunched
in a paper bag under my arm, the juggle
of food, briefcase, drink started to collapse.
It was around midday. I know the commuter
paths from the station, how to weave through
the concrete walkways, over roads in the spots
where traffic parts and lets you miraculously
through. These are the routes where the classic
people live, the ones who'll stick in my memory cells
even when the mind's shot, great blank slots of time
and visions revolving by turns like the movies.
They are the ones who ask me for everything
as I go by, every day, everything I have. One boy
leans against the wood palings he sleeps behind,
calling for change from his nest of blankets,
calling for my cup of tea, calling me love
as he crawls through the gap in the wood.
It's hard to stay perfect on that route, but
this day I was smiling at a lovely fantasy
until I slipped up on a piece of hamburger mashed
on the road, turning the juggle with my possessions
into a full stunt routine, legs, arms flying, the food
I was bound to waste at the end of it all. Then
the boy with the mad embroidery of muck
on his lapel stared me down again, daring me
to be bad. I offered him my apple and he turned
green, muttered, clasped his body in many places
and swung away. I sensed I was getting a tongue-lashing
and didn't want to ignore it, but I couldn't understand
a word. I put the food in a little pile in front of him,
the steaming tea, the papers, briefcase, all
the bags. I took off my coat, my shoes, every
piece of clothing and stood sweating in the light rain
but he didn't want me to know his language,
his eminence, his damnation or his delight.

OXFORD POETS

Fleur Adcock
Edward Kamau Brathwaite
Joseph Brodsky
Basil Bunting
Daniela Crăsnaru
W. H. Davies
Michael Donaghy
Keith Douglas
D. J. Enright
Roy Fisher
David Gascoyne
Ivor Gurney
David Harsent
Gwen Harwood
Anthony Hecht
Zbigniew Herbert
Thomas Kinsella
Brad Leithauser
Derek Mahon

Jamie McKendrick
James Merrill
Sean O'Brien
Peter Porter
Craig Raine
Henry Reed
Christopher Reid
Stephen Romer
Carole Satyamurti
Peter Scupham
Jo Shapcott
Penelope Shuttle
Anne Stevenson
George Szirtes
Grete Tartler
Edward Thomas
Charles Tomlinson
Chris Wallace-Crabbe
Hugo Williams